LOVE IS LIBERATION

KASHISH PALIWAL

I want to thank my mom and dad because they have always gave me the freedom to be who I want to be on both personal and professional levels. My mom is the person behind expanding the horizons of my imagination and creativity.

Thank You.

Contents

Contents

Preface

When I was fifteen, I wrote my first poem, and ever since then writing is my best friend. People come and go but ink and paper are my constant. It helps me heal and explore my deepest desires and wounds. Somewhere I always wanted to leave mark on this world, I guess this book is my mark.

1. A friend of mine.

A friend of mine
She wears classic red lipstick
And obsessed with heels
She writes poetries
About her heartaches
The stories in her head
Always have the dark ends,
Deeper than pacific
Mysterious like the dead ends
She talks with the stars
With the full moon, her cycle ends
She's criminal
Trap guys in love spells
They think she's innocent
But she tames the hell,
Katy, cries boys never stay
But she's always the first to leave
Don't look into her eyes
You will fall for false beliefs,
Dancing in the woods
She's the person
Locals warned you about
And her identity?
All her ex-lovers
Are still in doubt.

Her touch can heal you
Big eyes can hypnotize you
She will say, she doesn’t use her magic
To manipulate lives
But I'm here to warn you.

2. Slavery.

Hallucinated by the drug
Of my hopeless romanticism
Overdosed, I dig my own grave
No lover, No petal, empty slate
Bad love, I was a slave.
Twisted definitions, manipulated confessions
I was cuffed more than just in bed
Love start and ends in my head
A cruel mind was a hostage.
Sinking deep in the depths of the dead
No emotional availability, we had to act dead
The heat of bodies was hell fire, burnt my skin
In the club, dancing skeleton ;
Woke up in time, now wake up in grave
A small rose near my body
Gave hope to be alive again.

3. Invite me to hell.

He takes weed with breakfast
Producing beats, Audi is so fast
More than looks, he's such a vibe
Do want medicine to be alive?
Because I can sense, you're dead inside.
Baby, you caught my eye
You're such a type
Because I know you'll stay around during the bad time
And bedtime.
I see the halo over the devil
That's how I hide my evil
My urge to be bad
That's why I attract to the dead
I'm so weird
Cryptic mind
And this is what I love to find
Boy, you're what
I desire to be inside
That's why I want you beside
Over me, the dear devil
Worship me in your bed
Let me rule that head
Make me Bad
An angel from heaven, but a kind of rebel
Invite me to hell.

4. Yellow Magic.

Always been in the dark
You're a little too bright for me
Just when you smile like a child
You heal the child inside me,
Never imagined love is possible for me
But now when I see you beside me
I know I belong to somebody
There's a sweet place for me,
When I gaze stars with you from the balcony
I know you're aiming for infinity
How can I give an upper hand to my insecurities?
You handle me and my doubts so gently,
Make time for me even on your busiest days
Take me to your parents and dates
Every time I look at you and think I'm so grateful
This love is so meaningful,
With you, I made a journey from dark to light
You're so bright,
Just like yellow magic, sparkling
I'm healing
Replaced screams with comfortable silence
Disappointments with efforts and acceptance
Replacing our aggression with passion
Honey, we're healing
Came from houses where luxury hides a lack of love

Our "home" is made up of love
Yes, we brought here scars and fears
But when I see sunlight grace your face
In the morning, I can see how past mistakes are getting clear,
The way we don't give upon each other
And grow together
I'll hold on to you tight, this love is so bright
Replacing everything traumatic
With our love's yellow magic.

5. Venom.

Do you miss me on empty roads?
I used to walk around there
When I was a kid
And all those loud laughs
Over the swing
A small town, that is not visible on the map
Small girl, dreams and long naps
Zè, do you miss me while bleeding in a closet?
Dark days which you hated
And my house was haunted
So we picture ourselves under the bright sun
Running away from our demons
Where you introduced me to my venom.
Miss me when you look at the sky
I know you're still high
Concentrating on just i
You're a narcissist, don't deny
But I can skip this fact
Like I did when I was thirteen
I know your house is haunted too
So I still got the same warmth for you
I want good for you.
Two broke kids, whose fathers are screaming
And we try to find love, we crave for
But never got

Well, you used to think I don't understand
I know love is what we always wanted
Because our houses were haunted.

6. If it's my last day.

Ain't no fear to die
Ain't no motive to be alive
But if it's my last day
I'm gonna live it in this way:
I'll stare at you as I would stare at my last full moon
I'll laugh with you
And sleep in your arms till noon
Music is the way I've survived
So I'll give you my playlist to push rewind
I'll dance with you
Till midnight like I'm feeling the night sky for the last time
And suddenly the last day seems more beautiful than the rest of my life
Am I depressed or deprived?
It was always hardest to breathe around you
Maybe that's why it takes last breaths to be with you.

7. How will you kill a dead?

I want to love you anyway
Explaining dreams to potential walking nightmare
Making you my religion, potential criminal
But what can hurt me, I am already hurt
If you try to kill me, what can kill me
I am dead inside, I am so fearless
I am divine.
Love takes courage, I am tired of coward men
So if you are a desperado, love
Drunk, driving at one twenty, we are alive
Because we are not afraid to die, tonight I fly
Showcased vulnerability, we are courageous enough to cry
I love your harsh truths, so sick of lies
Hold my hand, I am not fine.

8. Don't contact me.

Buzzing phone, I don't need attention
Toxic environment or futile connections
No, don't wonder what I'm doing
Must be better, without you
Good on my own
In new town
Wine and new gowns.
Don't flirt with me, leave me alone
Don't be friends with me,
I'm trying to focus on my own -
Mess, I'm so stressed
Detoxing me.
Boundaries so high you gotta level up to contact me
Okay, listen, please don't contact me
Enough of controlling me, modifying me
Changed so much to fit in, became toxic and pathetic
(I am) maybe outcast but authentic.
Don't suggest clothes, don't make promises
Your intentions were right, but it had all damaged me,
Pretty badly.

9. Surrender to love.

Hold my hand
Let's run to the dead ends
Where life meets the death
I will make you feel alive,
Trippy smoke of your weed
Love more out of the box than it
And if you feel alienated too
Say, I'm into it
Rhythm of Damaged souls
Let's dance on it
Common love?
I don't want it,
We're designed for something phenomenal
When our stars - souls - bodies align it's a phenomenon.
Made of love, made for love
So why are we running from love?
Baby, we're designed to make love.
Shared naked body many times
Share your naked soul with me
Eye contacts, I know you're visionary
Uplifting our energies
feel the intensity
Crave for me
Even when you're having me
Love making in frequencies

Let your frequencies
Align with me.
Made of love, made for love
Tonight, surrender to love.

10. Vision 2030.

Wake up in the silk sheets
Baby, I hit the gym in the style
My skin is shining
Like my diamond ring,
Hair is stronger like my beliefs
And longer like my bills
ATM is my genie
I still love to enjoy freebies,
My closet is chic
Glorified by Fenty beauty kit
Lash and nail extensions
Baby, a girl like me never craves for your attention.
My four rings dominate the streets
Like I tower in my Gucci heels
Try to keep my ego slim
Like my body
Because bundles of cash are thick
Like my booty,
Unconditional love flows to me
Because I have a good karma
Before spending money in 5 stars
I feed a hungry person
Charity work in my therapy
My past is my lesson,
Then they ask me, Girl, what's your secret?

I say, welcome to my world
My crystals, My intentions
Gratitude journals, board of visions
I follow Moon patterns
To break my own patterns,
Meditation, Affirmations
I create what I like
And I like what I create
Step into your power
Never let your inner goddess hesitate
Just love yourself
And manifest.

11. I jumped in/with chaos.

Losing faith in everything
But I put faith & hope in your touch
When love feels like a teenage rush
I feel like in-mid thirties already, mentally
But your stare was almighty,
I always try to find intimidation
But you almost felt like home
Peaceful, nostalgic, and healing
So, I hold your hand & jumped in.
Waking up and watching you working with those specs on
How does it feel to be that beautiful?
Couldn't calm the hurricane inside that pretty head
But you put mine to a pause, maybe for a while
But paused, it was beautiful
Enjoying silence, sunlight, and breakfast, appealing
So, I hold your hand & jumped in.
Source of your affection and aggression
I remember making you the source of my adoration
Scented candle, diet cokes, and little longer naps
Longer routes to home, closing maps
I kept you like a secret, now you feel like a dream
You were a beautiful man, momma raised a gentleman
So, I hold your hand & jumped in.

12. Nancy.

The nostalgia of our childhood games, dancing to our favorite songs
Two 8 years old
Wearing my mom's clothes and jewelry,
Pranks, cursing boys who'd broken our hearts
Drinking, fake birthday party, and smoking at 2 AM
Two 21 years old,
And now it's part of our history
Are you thinking about us just like me?
Sometimes I pick up my phone to call
But it is not as simple as it used to be, I recall
Suffering and healing, I wish lessons were not this harsh
Making new friends was never this hard.
On the bright side, I'm becoming more me
New city, new achievements, I'm becoming who I am meant to be
But maybe, I'll always cherish the glory days of you and me
This is the fact with which I have made peace,
Now there's no parameter I have to fit in
More comfortable in my skin
I'm happier inside and I'm doing good
Fewer dudes, fewer hoods,
Our bond ran so deep within that it felt like a cage
Your city, those boys, memories were hostage,
Now maybe it's a little lonely
But I guess it's all good for me.

13. Thirty-eight yrs old.

He doesn't underestimate me
Doesn't treat me like his little girl
Instead gives me space to be a lady
Observing me dancing and dominating from a distance
In the crowd, he's my loudest applause,
Contemporary mindset even though my oldie is thirty-eight
Gentleman, the man of my dreams
Rudest man in the room, he only loves me
Stares at me like he owns me, like he's proud of me.
I'm done with confused boys, my man gives me stability
When he touches me, it's the warmth of security
With him, I'm becoming who I'm meant to be
He looks into my eyes, I hope he won't leave me
His touch is home to me.
I stand beside him, he helps me to feel taller
Shining bright under his glory, he never lets me feel smaller,
Views so feminist, firm opinions on politics
Apart from looks, his personality is significant,
He's a walking work of art, classy and modest
I didn't even exaggerate.

14. A poetry for you.

I saw you reciting poetry at sunset
The warmth of words protected me
The chaotic crowd, met a gala of rich kids
Your old jacket won the stage for me.
Something about your voice, I never forget it
Sad eyes, I see your demons, strangely
I'm not scared of it,
Country music you adore, I hear the longing for lover (in all of them)
What are you looking for? (in all of them)
Misery disguised in your words
Your thoughts are more puzzled than your curly hair
Still, I've never been so intrigued before,
Low self-esteem, you can't see how I see you
I wish you see yourself how I see you
So here is poetry for you.

15. An abandoned- cursed wonderland.

Maybe
I'll keep on missing you
You're first thought in the morning
Songs you used to vibe on
Play in my car
Like the national anthem
Of our reckless nation,
The fragrance of your perfume
Gives me a flashback of
Golden days, museum dates
Like Picasso, you painted me
In the colors of happiness, acceptance, and love
But now I'm standing lifeless
Like some sculptures,
You are everywhere
And still nowhere
Lost like a mirage, like you never existed,
We never existed,
There was peace with you
Silence without you screams so loud
Loudest, just how your demons are -
Ghosting my abandoned-cursed wonderland.

16. Urges of my feminity.

I do not want to dominate any man
I want to be your sweet little angel
Whole my lifespan,
Wearing clothes for you or nothing just for you
Multiple lovers? It's so typical 21st century
Let me marry you,
The divine feminine is upset by capitalism
My feminity is craving for baking cookies, planting a beautiful garden
And nourishing your mommy issues,
Echoes of my heartbeats scream for you
Like Luna's for her alpha, love at first sight
I feel like so out of order, your love can make me feel alright.
I don't want to be a man, manliness lacks the elegance
Do not fight with me, Go fight for me, I am your alliance
Want a man who can serve me with all his dominance.

17. Aiden Sullivan.

Aiden Sullivan,
If somebody has ever loved me then it is you
And I hope you know that I know,
Time with you was like living in the countryside
Out of world's sight
Where poets had fallen in love
And where sea waves echoes
Like living poetry in wine yards
We had it all,
Until you choose fireflies over the Sun
Until love felt like a cage and suffocated me
Until you wanted to keep me out of the world's sight
Because I was to keep at the side
We had it all.
You love me but you love yourself more
Now you left with all that money and foes
Being with you had always felt like home
I loved you too, I hope you know.

18. Romanticizing Loneliness. (don't keep a check on me, leave me.)

Something about this peace
That I‘m romanticizing this loneliness
Felt more love than he besides
Something healing inside
About my past, I’m gaining insights
Flights and delight.
Wearing floral dresses
He used to hate them
Reading more books
"How the efff do you like them?! "
Dancing in the rain, secretly
I'm in your city
Don’t keep a check on me, leave me
I want to be authentically me
Wine and star gazing on the balcony.
Don’t need a man, so good on my own
Decorating my place, on my own
I am clearing up all mess
Damsel is no more distress
I know you are annoyed to see me happy
So simply, don’t keep a check on me, leave me.

19. Spiritual Love.

I feel you like breeze on my skin
Among these knights
I know you're my King,
I always knew about your existence
Like God, never seen but faith
And I hold on to this belief
Like the untold dimensions of life,
Waiting from past nine years
I've lived you everyday
I've counted on you on my worst days
Wanted you on my best ones
During my eclipse
Your existence was the Sun.
The soul within recognises you like fingerprints
My energy field aches for it's twin,
Frequencies of your name echoes in my mind to wake me up from amnesia
Higher form of spiritual connection gives me nostalgia,
Praying on the altar, vow to surrender to the divine
Closed the eyes, opened third eye, let the stars align,
I trust the ideology of nirvana and purpose attached to love
I believe duality of oneself and lovers like Yin and Yang,
Like Devil, never seen but felt in faces and phases
And I hold on to this belief
Like the untold dimensions of death.

20. Open to love/ love myself.

In my private jet, I am with friends
My assistant said it is some celebrity over the phone
Got to attend parties in Paris
My lifestyle is lavish
Selected a dress from the Gucci store
They say it's bad for the rep to repeat a cloth
Walking in high heels, I've guards all around
But sometimes, in my Ferrari, I love to roam around
Well round ass, small waist
Every healthy meal on my plate
Most expensive watch on my wrist
Traveled everywhere on my bucket list
Kylie's shades on my lips
They ask me for tips,
Make millions every month
Donate 20 percent
Catch every eye with my style
Men are obsessed with my scents
But sometimes young money
Brings stress
So, converted the pool in my house
Into a bubble bath
Then watching Netflix with my lover, to ground myself
Being open to love and loving myself keeps me on the right path.

Why "love Is Liberation" ?

I started writing poetries when I was fifteen, thanks to stories and drama in my life, well having a heart always on my sleeves invited all of that. Life wasn't easy, my childhood wasn't like most people and hence, I developed demons.

Initially, back in 2018, I wanted to name the book 'ECLIPSED' but it would be about my demons, my relentless fight, it never happened, and I'm glad.

I fight for my freedom with myself, I loved my devil, I loved myself, and walked away from people I love to death just to honor my love for myself. It wasn't easy, and it will never be easy but always honor your love for yourself over every man and woman you love.

Acceptance is the key, I'll never fight with dark raging devils ever again, I'll invite them over a cup of tea and make them rest in peace. Accepting my dark side and loving it anyway will always be light at the end of every dark tunnel. That is why LOVE IS LIBERATION.

How Do I Get The Idea Of The Title? Pt. 1

Enter Caption

How Do I Get The Idea Of The Title? Pt. 2

On 07.01.2022, I took a break from work because I wanted to feel creative, didn't know what to draw or paint but I drew the painting with an ideology of having the essence of my spiritual journey in it. After painting it (ref. picture last page) I came up with the idea that love can provide you freedom.

Description: A man who was caught up in a matrix (labyrinth of suffering) but when love comes in (pink shade) came into the equation, the kiss of true love (lipstick stain) he is finally liberated from the web of the world. The chakras (blue and green shades depicting throat and heart chakras) are aligning slowly and the evolution of the soul is happening. Thus, love can liberate you.

This is how I came up with - "LOVE IS LIBERATION".

Thank You.

First of all, ***thank you*** for purchasing the book, right now I am drafting this book I do not know how many people will actually buy it, like it, or appreciate it but as you are reading this so thank you for buying and investing your time, energy and money in me, IT MEANS A LOT.

Hey!

I wanted to title this page as goodbye but in a true sense, it is just the beginning of you knowing me and connecting to me, so, HEY!

I would love to connect to you and know about feedback, it would be fun, I guess.

Blog - **KAY WRITES**

https://kaykp24.blogspot.com/

Podcast - **RANDOM TALKS WITH KAY**

https://open.spotify.com/show/0C323iR3VHCkXApsxSteYH?si=e4bbfbb88c8b4d70

LinkedIn - **KASHISH PALIWAL**

https://www.linkedin.com/in/kashish-paliwal-1870a91b1/?originalSubdomain=in

Instagram - **@ikashishpaliwal**

https://www.instagram.com/ikashishpaliwal/?hl=en

Printed by Libri Plureos GmbH in Hamburg,
Germany